SAFARI

# Giraffes

by Kari Schuetz

BELLWETHER MEDIA • MINNEAPOLIS, MN

Note to Librarians, Teachers, and Parents:

**Blastoff! Readers** are carefully developed by literacy experts and combine standards-based content with developmentally appropriate text.

**Level 1** provides the most support through repetition of high-frequency words, light text, predictable sentence patterns, and strong visual support.

**Level 2** offers early readers a bit more challenge through varied simple sentences, increased text load, and less repetition of high-frequency words.

**Level 3** advances early-fluent readers toward fluency through increased text and concept load, less reliance on visuals, longer sentences, and more literary language.

**Level 4** builds reading stamina by providing more text per page, increased use of punctuation, greater variation in sentence patterns, and increasingly challenging vocabulary.

**Level 5** encourages children to move from "learning to read" to "reading to learn" by providing even more text, varied writing styles, and less familiar topics.

Whichever book is right for your reader, Blastoff! Readers are the perfect books to build confidence and encourage a love of reading that will last a lifetime!

This edition first published in 2012 by Bellwether Media, Inc.

No part of this publication may be reproduced in whole or in part without written permission of the publisher. For information regarding permission, write to Bellwether Media, Inc., Attention: Permissions Department, 5357 Penn Avenue South, Minneapolis, MN 55419.

Library of Congress Cataloging-in-Publication Data
Schuetz, Kari.
  Giraffes / by Kari Schuetz.
    p. cm. – (Blastoff! readers. Animal safari)
  Includes bibliographical references and index.
  Summary: "Developed by literacy experts for students in kindergarten through grade three, this book introduces giraffes to young readers through leveled text and related photos"–Provided by publisher.
  ISBN 978-1-60014-604-6 (hardcover : alk. paper)
  1. Giraffe–Juvenile literature. I. Title.
  QL737.U56S38 2012
  599.638–dc22
                              2011007191

Printed in the United States of America, North Mankato, MN.

080111    1187

# Contents

# What Are Giraffes?

Giraffes are the tallest land animals in the world.

Spots cover
their bodies.
The spots get
darker as giraffes
get older.

Giraffes have long, blue-black tongues. The tongue is dark to protect it from sunburn.

Giraffes eat leaves from tall trees. Their favorite leaves are from **acacia trees**.

Giraffes must lower their bodies to drink. They spread out their legs to get closer to water.

# Predators

Crocodiles and lions **lurk** at **watering holes**. Giraffes must be careful!

Giraffes will kick **predators** when in danger. One kick can kill!

# Herds

Giraffes form **herds** to stay safe. Herds roam **savannahs**.

Males fight over females in a herd. They swing their necks and hit with their horns. WHAM!

# Glossary

**acacia trees**—trees with thorns that grow in savannahs

**herds**—groups of giraffes

**lurk**—to hide and wait

**predators**—animals that hunt other animals for food

**savannahs**—grasslands with very few trees

**watering holes**—natural areas filled with water; animals gather around watering holes to drink.

# To Learn More

## AT THE LIBRARY

Albee, Sarah. *Giraffes*. Pleasantville, N.Y.: Gareth Stevens Publishing, 2010.

Keller, Susanna. *Meet the Giraffe*. New York, N.Y.: PowerKids Press, 2010.

Ufer, David A. *The Giraffe Who Was Afraid of Heights*. Mt. Pleasant, S.C.: Sylvan Dell Pub., 2006.

## ON THE WEB

Learning more about giraffes is as easy as 1, 2, 3.

1. Go to www.factsurfer.com.

2. Enter "giraffes" into the search box.

3. Click the "Surf" button and you will see a list of related Web sites.

With factsurfer.com, finding more information is just a click away.

# Index